Is There Life on Other Planets?

And Other Questions about Space

GREGORY L. VOGT

ILLUSTRATIONS BY COLIN W. THOMPSON

LERNER PUBLICATIONS COMPANY

Minneapolis

Contents

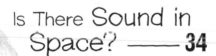

Perhaps you've heard these common sayings or beliefs about space:

The Moon is made of green cheese!
There's life on other planets!

But are these sayings true?

Is there any science behind the stories? Come along with us as we explore these old beliefs and more. Find out whether the stories and sayings you've heard about space are

FACT OR FICTION!

Are There Really UFOs?

YES. BUT HOLD ON A MOMENT THERE! Don't jump to conclusions. UFO means "unidentified flying object." That is a broad term. Anytime you see a flying object and don't know what it is, you are seeing a UFO. That UFO could be a bird, a plane, or a weather balloon.

OK, you're more interested in a particular kind of UFO. You want to know whether spacecraft from other planets have visited Earth, right? The answer to that question is, nobody knows.

Some people claim they have been kidnapped by aliens. But they never seem to have any proof that they have seen creatures from other worlds. And many people have reported seeing strange-looking UFOs. They say these were not weather balloons or airplanes. Could they really be alien spacecraft? The claims of the UFO observers are not easy to explain. Some of these observers show photos as proof. But pictures of UFOs are not proof of alien spacecraft. Just because you don't know what the flying object is doesn't mean that it came from another world.

Unless aliens from another world land on Earth and stick around to talk, we will always wonder: Are UFOs from other worlds? Or are they ordinary flying things that we just haven't identified?

FOIL

Is It True That There's No Gravity in Space?

Not sure about the answer? I bet you can answer this question: What keeps the Moon in orbit, traveling around Earth? You said gravity, right? **SO THERE *IS* GRAVITY IN SPACE!** Gravity is a force that attracts all objects to one another.

People often assume gravity disappears in space. **They think of astronauts floating inside their spacecraft. But gravity holds the spacecraft in orbit too! Otherwise, it would fly off into outer space, beyond the solar system.**

What about those floating astronauts? Rockets launch their space shuttle into space high above Earth. The moving spacecraft begins circling Earth. While it is going around in an orbit, it is actually falling.

Astronaut Stephanie Wilson floats (with a model spacecraft) on the space shuttle Discovery in 2007.

Inside, the astronauts are falling too. Because they are falling, they act as if gravity has gone away. But it hasn't.

Great Globs in Space!

Have you ever looked closely at a drop of water? Try it! It's more interesting than you think. Place a small drop of water on a piece of waxed paper. It looks almost perfectly round, right? Next, add some water to make the drop bigger. What happens? Does the drop look flat to you? If the drop looks flat, it's because big drops of water weigh more than little drops. And because of gravity, they take on a flat shape.

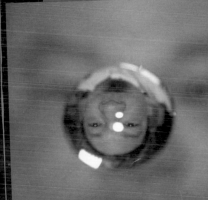

Astronauts like to play with water in space. Something different happens up there. The drops fall just like the spacecraft and the astronauts. So the water drops remain round no matter how big they get.

Do Astronauts Really Wear Diapers in Space?

YES! It sounds strange for space explorers to wear diapers. But it is necessary. Why?

NASA developed this space diaper, called a Disposable Absorption Containment Trunk, for women astronauts. It was used in space until 1988.

Well, during the countdown for a space launch, astronauts wear orange-colored launch suits. Their suits are heavy. They are made of many layers, which protect them in an emergency. One of the layers is made of rubbery material that holds air inside. A helmet that is shaped like a fishbowl completes the suit.

Toilet

Dressed in orange launch suits, astronauts approach the space shuttle *Endeavour* for a 2009 trip to the International Space Station.

It takes a lot of effort to put the suit on. If it weren't for a diaper, you know what would happen next. "Oops," one astronaut would say. "I have to go to the bathroom!" Off goes the suit. With seven astronauts on a mission, the space shuttle might never get launched into space.

Astronauts use diapers for space walks too. A typical space walk can last between six and eight hours. That's a long time to hold it. An astronaut may not like wearing a diaper. But when it's needed, he or she is glad to have it on!

Did You Know?

There is a closed-off area in a space shuttle called the waste collection system. In astronaut talk, that means "toilet." You go in there and urinate into a tube. The tube has a suction motor that works like a vacuum cleaner. (Don't try this at home!) You sit on a seat for solid waste. Air pulls the waste away from you into a tank below the seat.

Are the Sun and the Moon Really the Same Size?

NO. The Sun is much bigger.

This may sound like a silly question. Of *course* the Sun and the Moon aren't the same size! The Sun has to be bigger because its gravity holds the entire solar system together.

But actually, the question of whether the Sun and the Moon are the same size is not so silly. The Sun and the Moon look the same size from Earth. This is especially true during a solar eclipse. A solar eclipse is when the Moon passes directly between Earth and the Sun. When this happens, the Moon covers up the Sun exactly. (Important safety tip: Never look directly at the Sun during a solar eclipse—or at any other time! Sunlight can really hurt your eyes.)

OK, so what's going on during an eclipse? Why does the Sun seem to be the same size as the Moon?

The Moon appears to cover the entire Sun during a solar eclipse.

To find out, try this: Look at a tree that's growing somewhere off in the distance. Hold your thumb in front of your face. If you move your thumb just the right distance from your eyes, it looks as big as the tree. Of course, the tree is really a whole lot bigger than your thumb. But your thumb seems to be the same size because it's much closer to your eyes than the tree.

Let's go back to the Sun and the Moon. The Sun is 360 times wider than the Moon. But the Moon is 390 times closer to Earth than the Sun. The fact that the Moon is closer to Earth is what makes the Sun and Moon look the same size from Earth.

How Big Is the Sun?
The Sun is 864,000 miles (1.4 million kilometers) across. If the Sun were hollow, more than 50 million Moons would fit inside.

Is It True That Astronauts Become Weaker in Space?

YES! While astronauts are floating around in their spacecraft, they are also losing some of their strength. Their muscles don't get much of a workout. They can move from one place inside their spacecraft to another just by pushing against the wall with their fingertips. That's not good for their bodies. Muscles need exercise to stay strong. After two weeks in space, an astronaut will lose about 5 pounds (2.3 kilograms) of muscle!

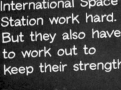

The crew of the International Space Station work hard. But they also have to work out to keep their strength!

Hard to believe? Here's an example to show you how it happens. Let's say you decide to do some strength training. An adult trainer encourages you to lift a 10-pound (4.5-kg) weight. It feels heavy at first. But after a few weeks of training, you have built up your muscles. So the weight seems lighter, and you move up to a 15-pound (6.8-kg) weight. But soon you get too busy with soccer to do any more weight

Astronaut Sunita L. Williams uses a special exercise machine on the International Space Station.

training. Weeks go by. One day you decide to lift that old 10-pound weight, and it feels ten times heavier! That's because when you took a break from weight training, you lost some or all of the muscle you'd built up. Astronauts lose strength in many of their muscles—not just the ones in their arms.

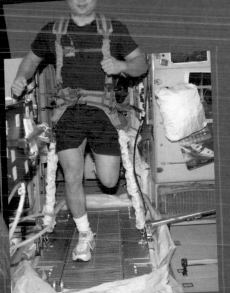

Did You Know?

To stay strong, astronauts in space exercise an hour or more every day. They run on a treadmill. And they also use big rubber bands for exercise. Astronauts attach the rubber bands to the floor of their spacecraft and pull on them. The exercise feels just like weight lifting on Earth. They also use the bands for stretching their arms and exercising their upper body.

Is There Really an Alien Face on Mars?

NO! You may be wondering why anybody would think this. Well, in 1976, NASA sent two unmanned spacecraft to Mars, a few months apart, to learn about the planet. As the spacecraft orbited Mars, a camera took a photo of a large mound of rock. The rock looked like a face. It had one eye, a nose, and a mouth. Surrounding the "face" was another layer of rock that looked like a really bad hairdo.

Some people believed the picture proved that there is life on Mars. According to these believers, Martians had carved the face. Scientists said the face was not real. It was caused by shadows. But the believers claimed NASA was lying.

NASA took this picture of the "face" on Mars in 2001. Does it look like a face to you?

About twenty years later, another spacecraft was accidentally destroyed just as it reached Mars. The face-on-Mars believers became angry. They claimed NASA destroyed its own spacecraft so it couldn't take any pictures of the face.

NASA said they wouldn't destroy their own spacecraft. A face carved by Martians would be exciting!

In 2001 still another spacecraft began orbiting Mars. It took a picture of the surface of Mars where the face appeared to be. This time, a better camera was used. The Sun was higher in the sky, and shadows were shorter. The face had disappeared! It had been the creation of shadows after all.

Were the face believers convinced? Nope. They claimed NASA used computers to change the picture and hide the face. Some myths never die.

15

Is There Life on Other Planets?

IT'S CERTAINLY POSSIBLE. No life has been discovered yet anywhere except on Earth. But other planets besides Earth might be able to support life.

Mars is one example. Mars is colder than Earth. But some parts of the planet are quite warm. On portions of Mars, it can get as warm as 70°F (21°C). Mars may also have water, which is necessary for life to exist.

NASA has sent many unmanned spacecraft to Mars to look for signs of life. Some examined Mars from their orbits to look for signs of water on the surface of the planet. Other spacecraft have landed on Mars and sent small robots with wheels to look for living things among the rocks. Eventually, human astronauts will land on Mars and continue the search.

There are still other places where life could exist.

Astronomers have discovered hundreds of planets circling other stars, like the Sun. They hope to find planets like Earth These planets would be good places to look for life.

Another place to look for life might be on the moon Europa. Europa orbits the planet Jupiter. It has an icy surface with an ocean of water below it. There could be living things swimming in Europa's ocean. Someday a spacecraft will go there and drill through the ice to the water below. The spacecraft will drop a small robot submarine in the water to do a little exploring.

This illustration shows a small robot exploring the surface of Mars.

Earthlike planets are hard to find. They need to be just the right distance from their stars. If they're too close, they would be way too hot for life to exist. And if too far, they would be much too cold. If scientists from the United States or another country find a planet with life, they might send it a powerful radio message: "Hello, anybody there?"

Does the Moon Really Rotate on Its Axis?

YES. It is easy to get fooled by the Moon. The same craters and the same large dark areas always face Earth. That's why many people think the Moon doesn't rotate.

So how can the Moon rotate while always showing Earth the same face? This happens because the Moon takes 27.3 days to make one orbit around Earth. And it takes the Moon about the same amount of time to make a complete rotation on its axis (the imaginary line running through the Moon).

Is this just an odd coincidence? Not really. Earth's gravity and the Moon's gravity pull on each other. This tug-of-war has slowed the Moon's rotation to the same number of days it takes to orbit Earth.

Try This!

It actually would not be possible for the Moon to show Earth the same face without rotating on its axis. To see why, have a friend stand in the middle of a room. Pretend you are the Moon and your friend is Earth. Walk in a circle around Earth to imitate the Moon's orbit. While you do, make sure you always face Earth. You can't really do this without turning your body, can you? To make a complete orbit of Earth, you must slowly rotate your body all the way around.

Whether you're standing on Mount Tengu in Japan (left) or in Montana in the United States (background), you will see the same face of the Moon.

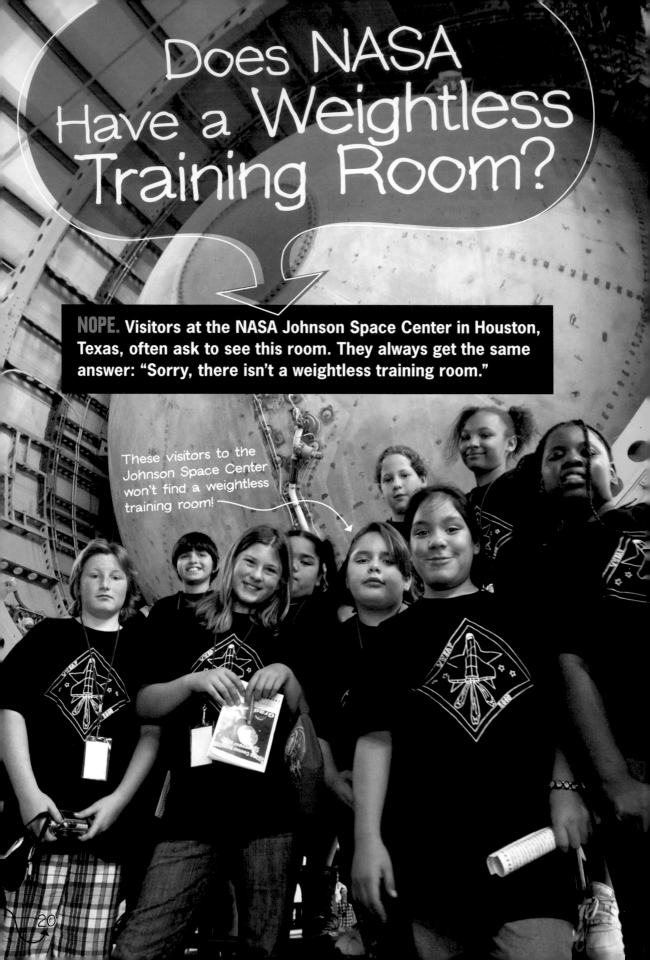

Does NASA Have a Weightless Training Room?

NOPE. Visitors at the NASA Johnson Space Center in Houston, Texas, often ask to see this room. They always get the same answer: "Sorry, there isn't a weightless training room."

These visitors to the Johnson Space Center won't find a weightless training room!

We get excited watching videos of astronauts in space. They tumble in the air and play with floating food. Somehow, people get the idea that there is a room where you push a button and gravity magically goes away.

Astronauts do have a place where they practice for spaceflight. It is a jet plane with most of the seats removed. The inside is padded. The plane flies a path like the track of a roller coaster. It quickly goes up and down many thousands of feet. As the airplane does so, the astronauts inside are tossed into the air. For a short while, the astronauts feel as if they are in space. They practice jobs they will do during their space missions. Then the pilots fly level and get ready to do it again.

Astronauts practice for an upcoming spaceflight aboard NASA's special jet plane.

The pilots repeat the roller-coaster ride in the air forty times before returning to the airport. Flying on the plane can be great fun for the astronauts. But not all of them like it. They have given the plane a nickname—the Vomit Comet. Bet you can guess why!

Underwater Training

Astronauts have another way to prepare for spaceflight. They train underwater. NASA has a large pool where astronauts train wearing space suits. Weights are added to the suits to keep the astronauts from rising or sinking in the water. This makes them feel as if they are in space. While underwater, astronauts practice fixing spacecraft.

Is It True That Astronauts Eat Freeze-Dried Ice Cream in Space?

THEY TRIED IT ONLY ONCE. In 1968 the three astronauts on the Apollo 7 mission had freeze-dried ice cream for dessert. It was a combination of strawberry, vanilla, and chocolate wrapped in a foil package.

The astronauts didn't like the ice cream very much. Although it tasted like ice cream, it became gooey in their mouths.

Freeze-dried ice cream was strange stuff indeed. To make it, workers placed regular ice cream inside a vacuum chamber. The chamber was a jar or box from which all air had been pumped out. The ice cream was heated inside the chamber. The frozen water in the ice cream turned into a gas, which was pumped out of the chamber. It took hours to remove all the water from the ice cream.

A NASA food technician puts a tray of fried rice into a freeze dryer. Astronauts' food is cooked fresh and freeze-dried at a laboratory in the Johnson Space Center.

By the time all the water was gone, the ice cream had become a dry brick. The astronauts didn't have to put it in a freezer. They could keep it in a pocket if they liked.

Someone thought freeze-dried ice cream would make a perfect dessert for spaceflight. But since the astronauts didn't agree, freeze-dried ice cream was never brought to space again.

An astronaut's silverware includes a pair of scissors. Space diners need to cut open the packets that contain their food. Velcro and magnets keep dinner from floating away.

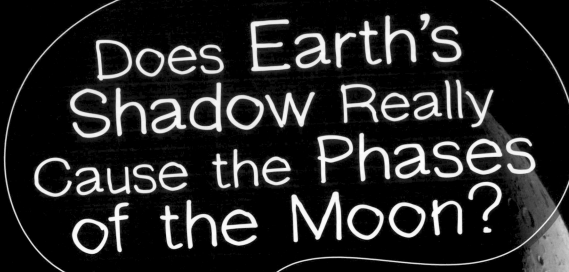

Does Earth's Shadow Really Cause the Phases of the Moon?

On some nights when the sky is clear, the Moon looks like a silvery slice of melon. Other nights it's a half circle. And about once a month, it's a round, shiny ball. **THESE ARE ALL PHASES OF THE MOON. AND THEY HAVE NOTHING TO DO WITH EARTH'S SHADOW.** So how does the Moon do these shape-shifting tricks?

Lunar Eclipse

You already know about an eclipse of the Sun. Did you know that sometimes there is an eclipse of the Moon? It's called a lunar eclipse. It occurs when the Moon passes into Earth's shadow. For an hour or two, the Moon seems to disappear. When the Moon leaves Earth's shadow, the eclipse is over. We can see the Moon again.

The Moon's phases are caused by its orbit around Earth. When the Moon passes between Earth and the Sun, the side of the Moon facing Earth is dark. It doesn't receive any light from the Sun. We call this phase the new Moon. When the Moon is on the opposite side of Earth, the entire side of the Moon facing Earth reflects the light of the Sun. It looks very bright. We call this phase the full Moon.

When the Moon is in other places in its orbit, some of the side facing us is lighted and some is dark. For example, when we see half the Moon lit up by sunlight and half in darkness, we call this a quarter Moon. That's because we're looking at only a quarter of the entire Moon. And when we see just a sliver of the lighted Moon, we call the phase a crescent.

As the Moon orbits Earth, it appears to grow and then shrink. It takes twenty-eight days to go through its phases.

Did Astronauts Really Land on the Moon?

Ever since the first Moon landing, some people simply could not believe that astronauts really landed there. They claimed the landings were a fake. They called the news reports a hoax.

Astronaut Buzz Aldrin stands on the surface of the Moon near the U.S. flag.

U.S. soldiers stationed in Vietnam in 1969 read about the first Moon landing in a newspaper.

Of course, astronauts really *did* land on the Moon. Between 1969 and 1972, twelve Americans set foot there. So why wouldn't some people believe it?

Many of those who denied the Moon landings pointed to what they thought were mistakes in the pictures of the astronauts on the Moon. For example, in one picture, taken during the Apollo 11 mission in 1969 *(left)*, there is a wrinkled U.S. flag extending straight out from a pole. It looks as if it is waving. The flag was placed there by

two astronauts, Neal Armstrong and Buzz Aldrin. The Moon landing doubters said the flag proved the landing never happened. There isn't any air on the Moon. How could the flag be waving?

The answer was simple. The flagpole had a small stick that stuck out at a right angle from the pole. This stick held the flag out so that the stars and stripes could be seen. The flag looked as if it was waving because it was creased. Why was it creased? That's easy. During the flight to the Moon, the flag had been folded in its container.

Does the Sun Burn Fuel to Make Heat and Light?

NO. The Sun doesn't burn fuel the way your furnace burns oil or gas to create heat during the winter. And the Sun doesn't burn fuel the way the giant electric generators burn fuel at your local power plant so your lights will go on._____

The Sun makes heat and light through a process called fusion. It takes place deep within the Sun. Here's what happens. The Sun is mostly made up of atoms of a gas called hydrogen. Several hundred thousand miles beneath the Sun's surface, there is a lot of pressure. The pressure is created by all the hydrogen atoms piled up on top of one another. This pressure generates an enormous amount of heat. Scientists think the temperature in the middle of the Sun is 27 million°F (15 million°C)! The heat and the pressure cause hydrogen atoms to change into atoms of another gas called helium.

When the Sun creates helium through fusion, it releases a lot of energy into space. Some of this energy reaches us on Earth in the form of sunshine.

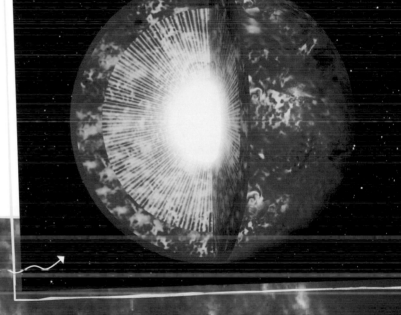

The surface of the Sun is much cooler than its center. But it's still a scorching 10,800°F (6,000°C)!

Did You Know?

The Sun fuses million of tons of hydrogen into helium every second! Even at that rate, the Sun has enough hydrogen to keep making heat and light for another four billion years.

Is It True That the North Star Never Moves from Its Place in the Sky?

NO. You'll find the North Star in the constellation called the Little Dipper. It's at the end of the Little Dipper's handle, almost directly above the North Pole. The North Pole is the northern end of Earth's axis. Earth rotates around this imaginary line.

This is the North Star. Can you see the shape of the Little Dipper? How about the nearby Big Dipper?

As Earth rotates, all the stars except one appear to move. Stars rise in the east, like the Sun, and set in the west. The one that doesn't seem to move is the North Star. To understand what is happening, stand in a room directly under a ceiling light. Slowly turn yourself in a circle. Everything around you appears to be moving. Now look up at the light as you turn. The light stays in the same place.

The North Star is like the light. The North Pole points at the North Star as Earth rotates.

This long-exposure photo shows the paths of stars in the night sky. The smallest, brightest circle is made by the North Star.

Even though the North Star seems to remain in the same place, it does move slightly. The star is not directly over the North Pole. So as Earth rotates, the North Star seems to swing in a tiny circle. But it does remain very close to the North Pole in the sky. So if you get lost at night, look for the North Star. When you face the star, you are facing north. If you face in the opposite direction, you are looking south.

Is There Sound in Space?

NOPE. When you watch your favorite space movie, you hear plenty of sound in space. You see the Star Wars character Luke Skywalker or Captain Kirk from Star Trek chase bad guys through the stars. Lasers, phasers, or photon torpedoes are fired. You hear guns go off and a whoosh or a buzz as energy beams streak through space to their target. A hit! Then comes the satisfying sound of the bad guys' spacecraft exploding.

We expect to hear sounds during a battle. That is why moviemakers put them in their films. But if you were watching a real space battle, there wouldn't be any sound.

What is sound, anyway? Sound is what we hear when something vibrates (shakes). Knock on a door. Hitting it causes the wood or metal to vibrate. The air around the door starts vibrating too. Atoms of air bounce against one another. The vibrations are carried from atom to atom until they reach your ears. Then the vibrations strike your eardrums, and you hear the sound.

If you shout out on Earth, lots of people can hear you. That's because there's air to carry the sound.

In outer space, there is hardly any air. So there is nothing to carry sound. That's why space battles would be silent—except for the bad guys. They would hear their ship being hit because there would be air inside it to carry the sound!

Is It True That the Moon Is Made of Green Cheese?

OF COURSE NOT! You knew that all along, didn't you? So what is the Moon made of? The Moon is actually a large ball of rock. Its surface is peppered with craters. The craters were made when space rocks struck the Moon's surface. You've probably seen a space rock at night. People often call them shooting stars because they seem to shine as they streak across the sky. The Moon has been struck by millions of these space rocks.

36

When space rocks strike the Moon, they crush some of the Moon's rocky surface and create Moon dust. The dust spreads everywhere. When astronauts have landed on the Moon, they've found the surface to be covered with this Moon dust.

Here's a wheel of new cheese. Its pale, bumpy surface looks like the Moon in the sky.

Now that you know what the Moon is really made of, you're probably asking yourself a question: Why the heck do people say the Moon is made of green cheese? Not only is the Moon *not* made of cheese. It's not even green!

Well, people say this as a joke. And they say it because they think the Moon looks a little like a newly made cheese wheel. Newly made cheese is called green cheese.

The Man in the Moon

The side of the Moon that faces Earth has many light and dark areas. If you stare at them long enough, you may be able to imagine the features of a man's face. Some people call him the Man in the Moon. In other parts of the world, the Moon's surface reminds people of a witch, a rabbit, or a scorpion.

GLOSSARY

astronaut: a person whose job is to fly through space

astronomer: a scientist who studies objects in outer space

atom: the tiny, basic unit that makes up everything, including you

axis: an imaginary line running through a spinning object, such as Earth

constellation: a grouping of stars that forms a pattern

eclipse: when one celestial body (such as the Sun) totally or partially blocks another celestial body (such as the Moon)

freeze-dry: a process that removes water from food so that it will last a long time

fusion: the process by which atoms of hydrogen are joined together in the Sun to make helium and release energy

gravity: the invisible force that causes all objects to be attracted to one another

helium: a gas made when hydrogen goes through fusion

hydrogen: a gas that makes up most of the Sun

Moon phases: monthly changes in the size and shape of the Moon as it appears to us on Earth

North Pole: the northernmost place on Earth. The North Pole is at the northern end of Earth's invisible axis.

orbit: the path of one object in space as it circles another object

spacecraft: any vehicle that travels in space

UFO: unidentified flying object

vacuum: a place where there isn't any air or gas present

SELECTED BIBLIOGRAPHY

NASA. "The Apollo Program 1963–1972." NASA Goddard Space Flight Center. November 24, 2008. http://nssdc.gsfc.nasa.gov/planetary/lunar/apollo.html (July 5, 2009).

———. "Astronauts Views of the Home Planet." Earth. N.d. http://earth.jsc.nasa.gov/sseop/efs/ (August 24, 2009).

———. "Photojournal." NASA Jet Propulsion Laboratory California Institute of Technology. N.d. http://photojournal.jpl.nasa.gov/index.html (July 5, 2009).

———. "Space Food." Human Spaceflight. November 25, 2003. http://spaceflight1.nasa.gov/living/spacefood/ (July 5, 2009).

Plait, Philip. Bad Astronomy. New York: John Wiley & Sons, 2002.

FURTHER READING

Everyday Mysteries
http://www.loc.gov/rr/scitech/mysteries/archive.html
Have you ever wondered what scientists mean when they say the universe is expanding? You'll find the answer to this question and many more at this fascinating website.

Google Moon
http://www.google.com/moon
Look at a map of the Moon, and see where each of the six Apollo space missions landed.

NASA
http://www.nasa.gov
Find out what NASA is doing at its official website.

Pogue, William R. How Do You Go to the Bathroom in Space? New York: Tom Doherty Associates, 1999.
This title by astronaut William Pogue answers 247 questions about living in space.

Waxman, Laura Hamilton. The Moon. Minneapolis: Lerner Publications Company, 2010. Waxman reveals true facts about the Moon in this interesting, photo-rich selection.

Woods, Michael, and Mary B. Woods. Space Disasters. Minneapolis: Lerner Publications Company, 2008. Read about some incredible space disasters in this fascinating title.

INDEX

ACKNOWLEDGMENTS

The images in this book are used with the permission of: NASA/GSFC, pp. 1, 16; © StockTrek/Stockbyte/Getty Images, pp. 2, 6; © Bruno Vincent/Getty Images, pp. 3 (left), 36; © Dennis Hallinan/Alamy, pp. 3 (right), 30–31; NASA/JPL/USGS, p. 4 (top); © PhotoLink/Photodisc/Getty Images, p. 4 (bottom); © Flirt/SuperStock, p. 5; NASA Human Spaceflight Collection, pp. 7 (both), 12 (inset), 13 (both); NASA/JSC, pp. 8, 21; Smithsonian National Air and Space Museum (A20000679000), p. 8 (inset); © Stan Honda/AFP/Getty Images, p. 9; © age fotostock/SuperStock, pp. 10–11; © Photodisc/Getty Images, p. 11 (inset); © NPA/Stone/Getty Images, pp. 12–13; © Science Source/Photo Researchers, Inc., p. 14; NASA/JPL/ MSSS, p. 15; NASA/JPL-SSV, p. 17; © SuperStock/SuperStock, pp. 18–19; © R. Creation/Sebun Photo/Getty Images, p. 19 (inset); © David Wei/Alamy, p. 20; © Todd Strand/Independent Picture Service, pp. 22 (both); AP Photo/Michael Stravato, p. 23 (top); AP Photo/Pat Sullivan, p. 23 (bottom); © Barry Blackman/ SuperStock, p. 24; © Larry Landolfi/Photo Researchers, Inc., pp. 25 (top), 27 (bottom); AP Photo/NASA, p. 25 (bottom); © iStockphoto.com/Rolf Meier, p. 26; © Joe Raedle/Getty Images, p. 27 (top); NASA, p. 28; AP Photo, p. 29; © M. Kulyk/ Photo Researchers, Inc., p. 31 (inset); © Robert Harding Picture Library/SuperStock, pp. 32–33; © Gerard Lodriguss/Photo Researchers, Inc., p. 32 (inset); Lucasfilm/20th Century Fox/ The Kobal Collection, p. 34; © Tom Merton/OJO Images/Getty Images, p. 35; © Heidi Wessman Kneale, p. 37.

Front Cover: © iStockphoto.com/Christian Anthony, © Antonio M. Rosario/Iconica/Getty Images (background).

Lerner Publications Company
A division of Lerner Publishing Group, Inc.
241 First Avenue North
Minneapolis, MN 55401 U.S.A.

Website address: www.lernerbooks.com

Library of Congress Cataloging-in-Publication Data

Vogt, Gregory.
    Is there life on other planets? : and other questions about space / by Gregory L. Vogt.
        p.   cm. — (Is that a fact?)
    Includes bibliographical references and index.
    ISBN 978–0–8225–9082–8 (lib. bdg. : alk. paper)
    1. Space astronomy—Miscellanea—Juvenile literature. I. Title.
    QB136.V64 2010
    500.5—dc22   2009020589

Manufactured in the United States of America
1 – JR – 12/15/2009